Liam's
BLUEPRINTS

A Double Donor Conception Story

Written by
SHARON LEYA

Illustrated by
JANNE MARU

Dedicated to the Jewish Fertility Foundation for their passionate work in building families— one unique story at a time.

With immeasurable gratitude to the donors, surrogates, medical professionals and scientists, who give so many intended parents a reason to believe in miracles. To my family and friends for their unending support over MANY years who were— all along— helping me write the story I was meant to tell.

And for my most precious little girl. May your life be filled with joy and pride, in not only who you are, but where you came from.

Sharon Leya

~VISIT WWW.MYDONORSTORY.COM FOR ADDITIONAL RESOURCES AND TO CREATE YOUR OWN PERSONALIZED, CUSTOM VERSION OF THIS STORY~

This book belongs to

· ·

Liam was excited about his first day of school!

Earlier that morning, Mommy had surprised him with a set of colorful building blocks to celebrate the special day ahead.

Liam loved building with blocks.

Liam and Mommy walked hand-in-hand through the neighborhood, looking at all the houses.

"Do you see that house?" Mommy asked. "I was the architect who designed that house."

Liam knew that Mommy was an architect, which meant she used her imagination to create all the instructions for how a house should be built... like what it would look like, where the doors and windows would go, and how tall it would be. Those instructions were called "blueprints."

Liam was very proud of his mommy. He decided he was going to use his new building blocks to build a house for his baby doll as soon as he got home from school!

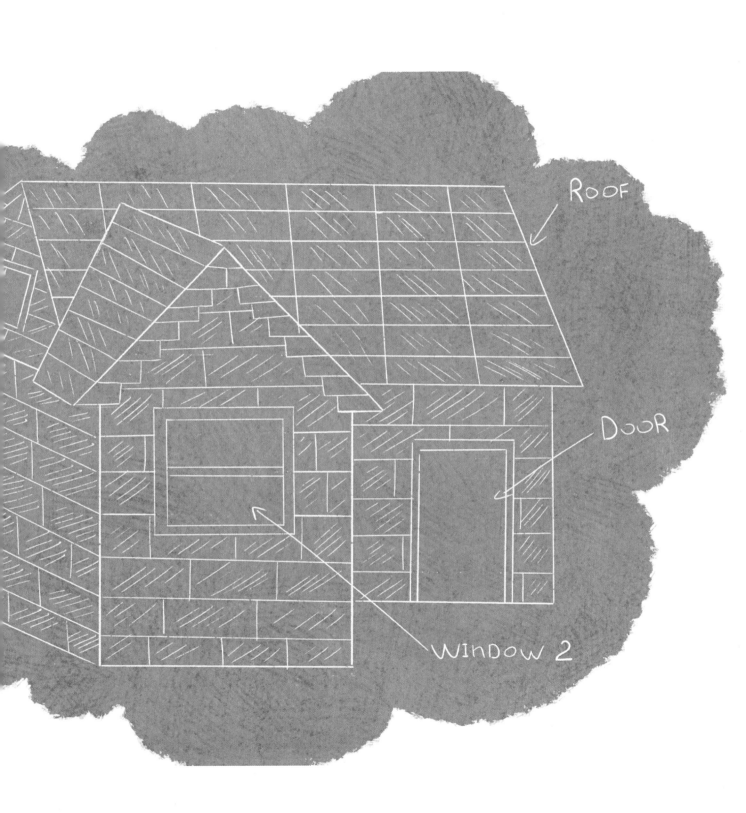

When Liam arrived at school, he saw his neighbor, Max, with his mommy and daddy.

"Guess what, Liam?" Max said. "I have a new baby sister!"

"Wow!" Liam replied. "Can I come see your baby sister soon?"

"Of course!" said Max's daddy.

"Where did you get the baby?" asked Liam.

"My mommy and daddy said they made her with lots of love and a little bit of science," said Max.

"Cool!" said Liam. And then he began to think.

Later that day, after a wonderful first day of school, Liam rushed home to play with his blocks. But he knew he had one big question he needed answered.

"Mommy," he asked. "Did you make me the same way Max's parents made his new baby sister?"

"I made you with a lot of love and a little bit of science, too," Mommy said. "But I also had some extra special help from two other people."

"What kind of special help?" Liam asked.

"Some people make a baby using donors," Mommy explained. "And that is how YOU were made."

"A donor? What is that?" Liam asked.

"A donor is a person who wants to help others grow their families," Mommy said.

"How do they do that?" Liam wondered.

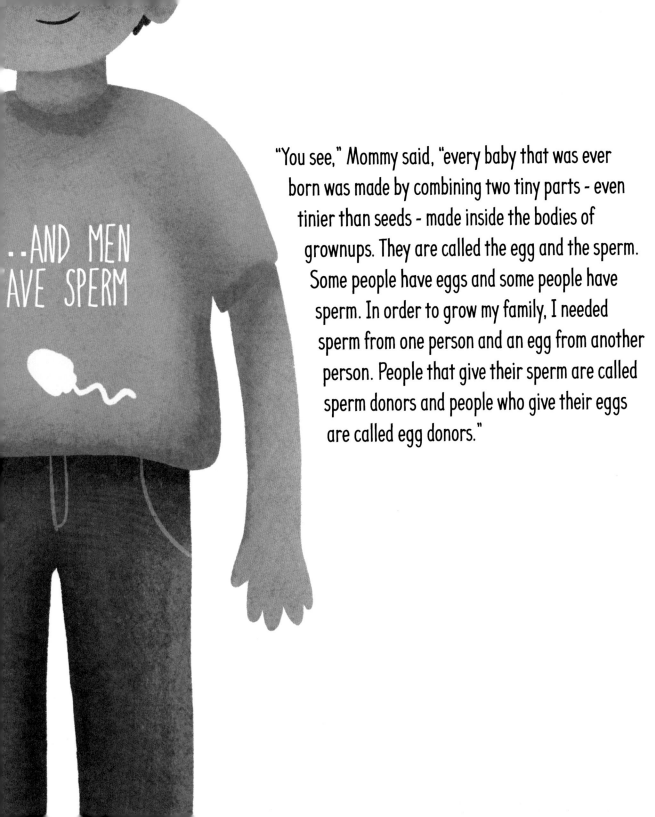

..AND MEN
AVE SPERM

"You see," Mommy said, "every baby that was ever born was made by combining two tiny parts - even tinier than seeds - made inside the bodies of grownups. They are called the egg and the sperm. Some people have eggs and some people have sperm. In order to grow my family, I needed sperm from one person and an egg from another person. People that give their sperm are called sperm donors and people who give their eggs are called egg donors."

"When I was ready to have a baby, a doctor put the egg and sperm together to create what is called an embryo. Then the doctor put the embryo in my uterus, which is like a cozy room right below my tummy where a baby can grow. That embryo became you! You grew for many months until you were ready to be born."

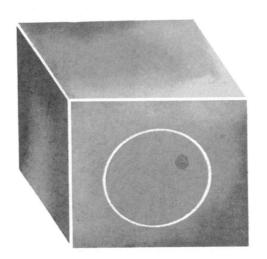

"Now," Mommy added, "every sperm and egg that come together has special instructions for how that baby will look, how tall they will grow and where all the parts should go."

"You mean... like blueprints?" Liam asked.

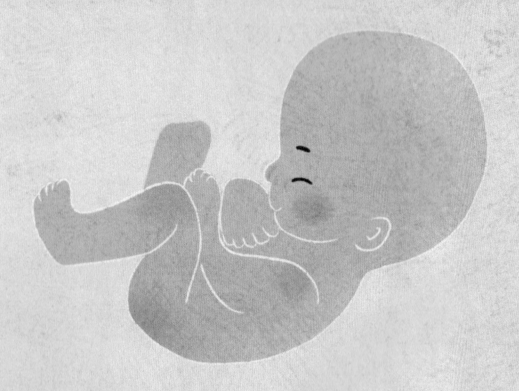

"Exactly!" said Mommy. "Or maybe we should call them 'YOU' prints!" Mommy and Liam giggled.

"Sometimes you need other people to help you with the blueprints. You got your blueprints from the donors. But who you are is so much bigger than your blueprints. You have my smile and my laugh and you love science just like your Grandpa."

"So even though I got my blueprints from the donors, my mommy is what built me!" Liam said with a big smile.

"Yes! I am so very grateful to the donors for giving me the blueprints to make YOU."

Liam began to play with his blocks again.

"But love is how you build a family, right Mommy?" Liam asked.

"That's right, Liam!" said Mommy as she reached over and gave Liam a giant, warm hug.

MY FAMILY

DISCUSSION GUIDE

In these modern times, family building is no longer confined to the traditional means of the past. Families are being created with the help of cutting-edge science, and donor conception is an increasingly common and more socially acceptable approach to bringing children into the world.

As recipient parents, you are part of a new generation of families learning how to deal with delicate and ever-expanding topics like genetic family trees, ethnicity, and identity.

While it is encouraged to educate your child on the uniqueness of their conception, it's also just as important to remind your child that ALL children have a special story to tell about how they came into being - from conception to birth and beyond.

Kids are naturally curious and love to hear and learn about how they were created. This discussion guide is designed to help support the conversations you might have with your child about their story - after reading Liam's story.

JEWISH
FERTILITY
FOUNDATION

There is a wide range of curiosity levels among donor-conceived kids. Your child may want to know the donor's name and where they live.

Wanting to have concrete information about your genetic parent is very normal and integral to the development of personal identity. You can support that desire with as much information as you have about the donors.

Explain to your child that some people know their donors, some meet them later in life, and some never meet their donors. Some donors choose to be anonymous, to keep their identity private. Some donors agree to contact once the child is 18.

There is also a wide range of opinions among donor-conceived people about whether a donor should be considered a "real" parent. Many donor-conceived adults feel that it is important to not dismiss a donor as simply a source of genetic material, but rather allow them to be recognized as a "real parent," a "genetic parent," or a "biological parent."

Other donor-conceived adults feel it is perfectly fine to de-emphasize the role of the donor in the child's life and simply refer to them as a donor.

Though the answer you choose to give may cause you to feel complicated emotions, it is still crucial to allow your child to define family however they choose to do so - whether it's through genetics, love or both.

"WHAT DO MY BLUEPRINTS LOOK LIKE?"

Your child may be curious about the donor's ethnic background and ancestry. They may ask whether the donor shares the same ethnic background as they do or ask about their heritage or race.

It is so important to validate your child's questions and let them know what you can share. Parents can explain how and why they chose a particular donor and include details about the donor's physical characteristics or ethnic background. You might find it helpful to create a notebook with personal details and photos of the donor to share with your child when you or they feel ready, or even teach them about their ancestral culture.

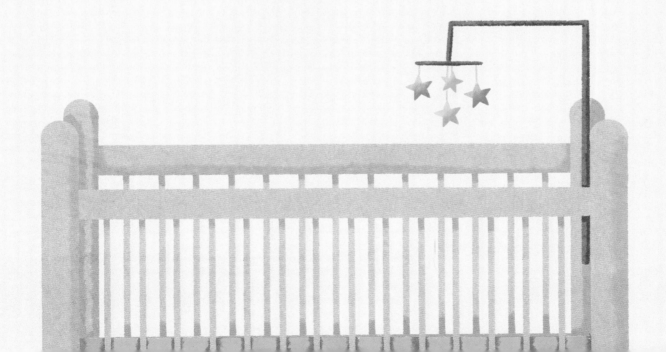

"DOES THE DONOR KNOW ABOUT ME? CAN I TELL PEOPLE ABOUT THE DONOR?"

As parents, it is important to teach your child the difference between privacy versus secrecy. Secrecy connotes "hiding," which children often interpret as something that carries shame and negativity, while privacy allows for a person to decide for themselves when and if to share aspects of themselves with others. You can explain that their conception story is private, which means it does not have to be shared, but that they have a right to their story and to discuss it as they see fit. From a donor perspective, you can explain that donors often want to help others, but they also may be private about becoming donors and do not necessarily want to share their identity for similar reasons.

It is very common for children to ask about other biological relatives, and this interest usually presents more in adolescence as children mature in their understanding of conception and genetic relationships. Donor-conceived kids are especially interested in half-siblings they may have. As parents, you can support, nurture, and normalize their curiosity. You can also form relationships with the families of their half-siblings through donor-sharing platforms, such as the Donor Sibling Registry, or by reaching out to your clinic.

The emphasis and central message for your child is how much they were wanted. As a parent, you dreamed, planned, researched, explored, and invested countless resources, all in an effort to realize your dream of creating your family. But also allow your child the space to feel any negative emotion attached to their conception story. After all, no matter how badly they were "wanted," a child might feel guilt or shame for experiencing resentment, confusion, or mixed feelings. Validate the normalcy of any and all emotions that arise.

Above all else, embrace your child's curiosity. While you have written the beginning of their story, the rest of the story is theirs to write!

Shubha Swamy, LPC, owner Novo Psychotherapy

On behalf of the Jewish Fertility Foundation

www.novopsychotherapy.com

www.jewishfertilityfoundation.org

More in the BLUEPRINTS collection

Visit www.mydonorstory.com to find the book that matches your family type or create your own personalized version.

Single Moms By Choice Families

Lilly   Liam

Single Dads By Choice Families

Eli   Emmy

Pick your conception type

Mom & Dad Families

Remy   Noah

Sperm Donor
Embryo Donor
Double Donor
Egg Donor

Two-Dad Families

Kaleb   Kenzie

Two-Mom Families

Maisie   Hudson

OR CUSTOMIZE YOUR OWN VERSION

Your child's name here

Made in the USA
Las Vegas, NV
24 October 2024